OUR COUNTRY, OUR WORLD

WRITTEN BY
CHRISTOPHER YEATES

COVER AND ILLUSTRATIONS BY
ZOE SADLER

© Gresham Books 2016
Published by Gresham Books Limited
The Carriage House, Ningwood Manor, Ningwood,
Isle of Wight PO30 4NJ
ISBN 978 0 946095 77 3

WHAT'S INSIDE

BRITISH VALUES

Britain is made up of England, Wales and Scotland, and the people who live in these countries are called **British**. The people of Northern Ireland may also call themselves British and together we make up the **United Kingdom**. This book is to help you learn about and come to understand some of the British Values we all share.

LET'S FACE IT: YOU'RE UNIQUE

It's pretty amazing to think that nobody else in the whole world has exactly the same thoughts as you or has exactly the same family and friends as you do, and nobody else in the world knows exactly what it's like to be you.

Everybody in the world is a little bit different to everyone else, and this makes them unique. This means that you are unique too, and for that you should be very proud.

Everyone in our country, and everyone in our world, is a little bit different. This makes everyone unique, and everyone very important. Yes, even the ones who sometimes get on your nerves, or who have different opinions to you.

In fact, everybody is equally important. We call this idea *equality*.

Equality makes sure that everybody is treated *fairly*, and has the same opportunity to make the most of their lives and special talents.

Always remember – everyone is **different**.
Everyone is **unique**.
And everyone is **important**.

What we mean when we say...

Equality: where everyone is treated the same and enjoys the same rights and opportunities.

Fair: treating people in the same way without favouritism.

Your turn to speak

With your partner:

→ Spend a few minutes looking very carefully at each other. Make a list of the ways that you and your partner look both the same AND different from one another.

→ Discuss together what you think it would feel like if people did not treat you as important and special.

Read and understand

1. Draw a picture of yourself.

2. In your own words explain why you think it is important that you should treat other people as important and special.

WHAT IS A CULTURE?

A *culture* is the ideas and traditions of a group of people who share a similar background, and do similar things together. Everybody is part of a culture. In fact, many people are part of more than one culture.

Your culture is made up of everything to do with how you live:
→ Your ideas and beliefs.
→ Languages you speak at home and at school.
→ The way you dress.
→ Religious faith.
→ Music you enjoy listening to, or the films or television programmes that you watch.
→ Sports you like playing.
→ The sort of food you eat.
→ Your history and the traditions you follow.

A *tradition* is a way of doing things that has been done before and comes to be accepted. All of these different things make up your cultural background.

Having lots of different cultures existing side by side makes our country an incredibly exciting, interesting place to live.

'Multi' means 'lots of'. Britain has lots of different cultures, so it makes sense to say that Britain is multicultural.

What we mean when we say...

Culture: the ideas, traditions and activities of a group of people.

Tradition: the passing on of stories, skills and ways of life from generation to generation.

Your turn to speak

With your partner:

→ Can you make a list of some of the special traditions you might have in your family. For example, your family might always have a special family meal together on birthdays or other family celebrations.

Read and understand

1. Draw a picture of an important event for your family. This could be your family celebrating a special religious day, or perhaps someone's birthday. What kind of clothes is everyone wearing? Is special food being prepared and eaten?

2. In your own words write about some of your family's traditions. Are there things that your family always does? For example, do you always go and see a fireworks display on Bonfire Night?

MULTICULTURAL FOR OVER 2000 YEARS

The *United Kingdom,* or UK, is made up of England, Wales, Scotland and Northern Ireland. Some people think that it is only recently that the UK has had lots of different people and cultures. This is not correct.

Our country has been multicultural for a very long time – well over 2000 years, in fact. Long ago in our island's history, the many *Iron-Age tribes* who lived here were from a lot of different cultures. Some of these tribes were called *Celts*, but there were others from all across Europe.

Then the *Romans* invaded, around 2000 years ago, and our country was changed forever. For the next 1000 years, invasions by *Anglo-Saxons*, *Vikings* and, in 1066, the *Normans* continued to mix many different cultures from all over Europe together.

Each of these groups had different languages, buildings, laws, faiths and traditions. Amazingly, the ways of life and ideas of these ancient people still play a very active part in many of our own cultures today.

What we mean when we say...

United Kingdom (UK): England, Wales, Scotland and Northern Ireland.

Britain: the island of Britain made up of England, Wales and Scotland.

Iron-Age Tribes: the many different tribes who lived in Britain during the Iron Age.

Romans: a powerful people who controlled a huge empire. They ruled England for about 400 years.

Anglo-Saxons: tribes from Germany, Holland and Denmark who lived in Britain from around 410 to 1066 AD.

Vikings: fierce raiders and traders from Scandinavia

Normans: in 1066 they invaded England, led by William the Conqueror, who thought he should be King of England.

Your turn to speak

With your partner:

→ Can you make a list of the different groups of people who came to Britain? Start with those who lived in Britain first.

Read and understand

1. Research and then draw a picture of one of the groups who have lived in Britain during the past 2000 years.

2. Which group invaded and conquered Britain in 1066? Who was their leader?

3. Make a poster giving details of the different groups who have lived in Britain.

OUR MULTICULTURAL UK

Lots of different people and cultures mixing together in the UK is nothing new. Some people arrived as *refugees*. A refugee is somebody who has been forced to escape their own country because it is not safe for them to live there. Other people arrived in Britain as *migrants*. A migrant is somebody who moves to another country to live and work there.

Since the Second World War, many migrants have come to Britain from *Commonwealth* countries. The Commonwealth is made up of 53 countries that used to be part of the British Empire before they gained independence. Migrants came from India, Asia, Africa, the West Indies and lots of other places all over the world.

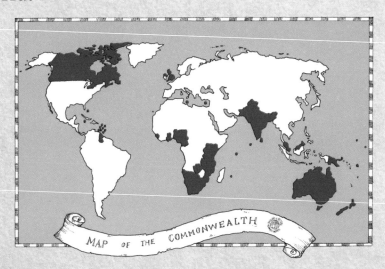

MAP OF THE COMMONWEALTH

Everyone who has settled in Britain has brought their special cultural backgrounds to share with the multicultural society that already existed here. Today, there are at least 300 different languages spoken in London every day!

What we mean when we say...

Refugee: somebody who has been forced to escape their own country because it is not safe.

Migrant: somebody who moves to another country to live and work.

The Second World War: the biggest and most damaging war in history, fought between 1939 and 1945.

The Commonwealth: a group of 53 countries across the world which used to be part of the British Empire before they gained independence.

Your turn to speak

A refugee is someone who has to leave their own country because it is not safe to remain there. Discuss with your partner:

→ What do you think it would be like to live in a country where a war is being fought?

→ Why do you think that wars cause a lot of people to become refugees?

Read and understand

1. How many countries are in the Commonwealth?
2. Explain in your own words:
   → What is a refugee?
   → What is a migrant?
3. Where have some of Britain's migrants come from?
4. Draw your own picture of the Commonwealth showing some of its 53 countries.

HOW DOES RELIGION HELP SHAPE OUR CULTURE?

Religion can be an important factor in a person's cultural background. In Britain, the biggest religion is Christianity, with a number of different denominations (or branches) such as Anglicanism (the official religion of England) and Catholicism making up the church as a whole. The next biggest religion in the UK is Islam, followed by Hinduism, Sikhism, Judaism and Buddhism.

Being an active member of a religious community is likely to play a big part in your daily routine, in the way you treat others, and the way you think about the world around you.

Even if you follow no religion at all, you might be surprised how much of your cultural background would be very different without the traditions that come from special religious days in our calendar.

Whether you know it or not, you have probably taken part in a number of Christian festivals and traditions.

You may well have eaten pancakes on Pancake Day. Pancake Day is on Shrove Tuesday, traditionally the day when Christians used up foods that they would not be eating during Lent. Lent is the 40 days before Easter when Christians believe that Jesus went into the desert to fast and pray. Lots of people give things up for Lent – like chocolate.

Easter is the most important celebration in the Christian calendar. For Christians, Easter celebrates the day when Jesus rose from the dead, three days after he died on the cross.

It can be easy to forget that Christmas is a religious festival, one of the most widely celebrated in the world. You may have had an 'Advent calendar' counting down the long days to Christmas Day, and you have probably sent Christmas cards to your friends or received presents at Christmas time.

Christmas Day celebrates the birth of Jesus in Bethlehem, over 2000 years ago.

What we mean when we say...

Denomination: a religious group that has slightly different beliefs from other groups that share the same religion.

Christianity: the religion based on the life and teachings of Jesus Christ.

Anglicanism: a form of Christianity and the official religion of England.

Catholicism: a form of Christianity and the faith and teachings of the Roman Catholic Church.

Hinduism: the main religion of India which includes worshipping many gods and the belief that after you die you return to life in a different form.

Sikhism: a religion founded in the 15th century in northern India, believing in one God.

Judaism: the religion of the Israelites of the Bible and of the Jews of today. Jews believe in one God, whose 'Chosen People' are the Jews.

Buddhism: a religion founded by Siddhartha Gautama in North-East India in the 5th century BC.

Your turn to speak

Even if you are not a Christian you may have taken part in a number of Christian festivals and traditions. Discuss with your partner:

→ Have you taken part in any Christian festivals and traditions? (For example, have you eaten pancakes on Shrove Tuesday? Do you send Christmas cards or go to church on special religious days like Christmas Day?)

→ Have you given up anything for Lent? Why do you think it might be a good idea to give up things sometimes?

Read and understand

1. Which is the biggest religion in Britain?
2. What kind of food are you likely to eat if you celebrate Shrove Tuesday?
3. Describe what Christians believe about Lent.
4. Describe what Christians believe about Easter.
5. What do Christians celebrate on Christmas Day?

RAMADAN

There are over two and a half million Muslims in Britain. Every year during the sacred month of Ramadan, Muslims give up food and drink during daylight hours. This is called fasting.

Ramadan is the fourth of the Five Pillars of Islam. For Muslims, fasting for at least 29 days is a very spiritually rewarding tradition, and one that many look forward to throughout the year.

Ramadan is a special month for Muslims because they believe it is the month in which the Prophet Muhammad began to have the Qur'an revealed to him. The Qur'an is Islam's holy book. The night that the Angel Gabriel first spoke to Muhammad is celebrated during a festival called Laylat al-Qadr, or 'The Night of Power'.

The end of Ramadan is marked by a joyous celebration called Eid al-Fitr – the Festival of the Breaking of the Fast. On this day, Muslims attend special prayers at their mosque.

To celebrate their first daytime meal in a month, Muslims invite friends and family round to help them eat their way through a huge banquet of curries, samosas, pakoras, kebabs and Kaek al-Eid – known to others as cookies!

What we mean when we say...

Ramadan: the ninth month of the Islamic year, during which Muslims fast from dawn to sunset.

Prophet: a special messenger who is sent by God to teach people how to live good and obedient lives.

Fasting: not eating or drinking.

Mosque: a Muslim place of worship.

Qur'an: the Islamic holy book believed to be the word of God as told to the Prophet Muhammad by the Angel Gabriel.

Five Pillars of Islam: the five practices that every Muslim must follow in order to live a good and responsible life according to Islam.

Islam: the religion of Muslims.

Laylat al-Qadr, or 'The Night of Power': the night that the Angel Gabriel first spoke to the Prophet Muhammad.

Eid al-Fitr: the Festival of the Breaking of the Fast which marks the end of Ramadan.

Your turn to speak

Discuss with your partner:

→ Have you ever given up food or drink for a while? How did it make you feel about the foods you gave up? Did it make you appreciate them more?

→ How would you organise an Eid al-Fitr celebration, and who would you invite?

Read and understand

1. Mosques are the holy buildings where Muslims go to worship. Draw your own picture of a mosque.

2. Roughly how many Muslims are there in Britain?

3. For how many days should a Muslim fast during Ramadan?

4. Make a fact sheet explaining what happens during Ramadan.

DIWALI

Every year, *Diwali* is one of the biggest festivals in the world and is important to a number of different religions including *Hinduism* and *Sikhism*.

Diwali celebrates the triumph of good over evil, and light over darkness.

The word 'Diwali' means 'rows of lighted lamps', and this festival is also called the Festival of Lights.

Diwali usually falls in October or November, and lasts for five days, with the fourth day marking the Hindu New Year.

To symbolise this, Hindus and Sikhs light up their houses and streets with candles (*diyas*), and light up the sky with fireworks.

Fun fact: One of the biggest Diwali celebrations in the world outside India takes place in the city of Leicester, in Britain's East Midlands.

What we mean when we say...

Diwali: means 'rows of lighted lamps'. It is one of the biggest religious festivals in the world and is celebrated by a number of religions including Sikhism and Hinduism. Diwali celebrates the triumph of light over darkness.

Diyas: candles.

Hindu: someone who practises Hinduism.

Sikh: someone who practises Sikhism.

Your turn to speak

Discuss with your partner:

→ The Festival of Diwali celebrates the triumph of good over evil or light over darkness. Why do you think people celebrate it with candles or fireworks?

Read and understand

1. Draw your own picture of a Diwali celebration; this might be candles lighting up a house or a firework display.

2. When is Diwali celebrated and by whom?

3. What does Diwali celebrate?

PASSOVER: A SPECIAL TIME FOR JEWS

Passover is one of the most important festivals in the Jewish year. The Passover Festival helps Jewish people remember how the Children of Israel left slavery when Moses led them out of Egypt over 3000 years ago.

During Passover, Jewish people spend as much time as possible with family and close friends. There are also special feasts called *Seders*.

Six foods make up the traditional Seder meal, and each helps Jews to remember the Passover story:

➜ A lamb bone, to recall the lambs sacrificed.
➜ An egg, to symbolise sacrifice.
➜ Bitter herbs, to represent the bitterness of slavery.
➜ Green herbs, to represent new life.
➜ A nut and fruit paste (charoset), to represent the mortar slaves worked with.
➜ *Matzo*, the bread of both slavery and freedom.

Everyone drinks four cups of wine (or grape juice) to symbolise the joy of God rescuing the Israelites from slavery.

To remind themselves that they are no longer slaves, everyone at the Seder sits on a comfortable cushion. The Passover story is retold from a book called the *Haggadah*.

What we mean when we say...

Passover: the Jewish festival that remembers the Exodus, the deliverance of the Israelites from slavery in Egypt.

Matzo: unleavened bread, that is crispy and looks like a biscuit.

Exodus: the departure of the Israelites from Egypt.

Seder: a special ritual dinner for the first two nights of Passover.

Haggadah: the book which is read aloud at the Seder which includes the story of the Exodus.

Your turn to speak

At Passover, Jews eat a number of special foods. Discuss with your partner:

➨ Why do you think eating special foods helps remember special events?

Read and understand

1. People from which religion celebrate Passover?
2. Who led the Children of Israel out of Egypt?
3. What is the name of the special Passover feast?
4. Why does everyone at the feast sit on a cushion?

FAMILIAR PATRON SAINTS

England, Scotland, Wales and Ireland each have special patron saint days. On these days, the *patron saint* is remembered and different parts of the national culture are celebrated.

St George – Patron Saint of England

St George's Day, celebrated on 23 April, is a special day to celebrate St George and the values he represents of English ideals of honour, valour and gallantry. On St George's Day, it is custom to wear a red rose, the emblem of England.

St George's personal emblem is a red cross which is also the English national flag. People fly the English flag to show their support for England.

St George is usually shown on horseback slaying a dragon, a legend used to inspire English knights during the Hundred Years War against France, in the Middle Ages.

St George is remembered in church services on the Sunday closest to 23 April. These services often include the hymn 'Jerusalem', written by the poet William Blake.

St David – Patron Saint of Wales

On 1 March, people in Wales celebrate Welsh culture and the life of their patron saint, St David. St David lived around 1400 years ago as a Celtic monk, who travelled widely across Wales to spread Christian ideas.

To celebrate St David's Day, people might attend a special church service, colourful parade, or traditional *eisteddfod* – a festival of Welsh poetry and music.

They eat a lot of *cawl* (leek soup), and take care to pin a *daffodil* or *leek* to their clothes, as these are both Welsh emblems. It was St David himself who issued the famous advice to Welsh soldiers fighting the Saxons, to stick a leek in their cap so they could tell friend from foe – clearly a handy tactic, as the Welsh won the battle!

St Andrew – Patron Saint of Scotland

St Andrew's Day is celebrated on 30 November, and is a day for celebrating the best of Scottish food, music and dress.

St Andrew was the first of Jesus Christ's twelve disciples. The bones of St Andrew are believed to have been brought to Fife, on the Scottish coast, where today the town of St Andrews stands. Like Jesus, and also St George, St Andrew died a *martyr*, crucified by the Romans on a diagonal cross called a *saltire*.

Today, the St Andrew's Saltire is Scotland's national flag, and is flown on St Andrew's Day. St Andrew's Day celebrations might include a *ceilidh* dance, probably to the accompaniment of *bagpipes*. It is also a good time for a taste of Scotland's national food: *haggis*, a special meat dish.

St Patrick – Patron Saint of Ireland

On 17 March, the people of Ireland and the Irish around the world wear their greenest finery and celebrate St Patrick's Day. St Patrick's Day is celebrated with parades, dancing and special foods.

St Patrick brought Christianity to Ireland. He was born in Roman Britain, but was kidnapped by Irish pirates when he was 16 and taken to work in Ireland as a slave for six years. He escaped back to his family, but later returned to Ireland as a priest and missionary.

It is said that St Patrick used a *shamrock*, a three-leaved plant, to explain the Christian Trinity of the Father, the Son, and the Holy Spirit. Today, the shamrock is the national flower of Northern Ireland, and the green plant is worn on St Patrick's Day.

St Patrick's Day is celebrated in more countries around the world than any other national festival. Americans even have the tradition of pouring vegetable-based dye into the Chicago River to turn it completely green.

What we mean when we say...

Patron Saint: a saint who guides or protects.

Valour: great courage in the face of danger.

Gallantry: bravery and consideration for others.

Eisteddfod: a festival of Welsh poetry and music.

Cawl: leek soup.

Saltire: a diagonal cross in the shape of an X, used as the national emblem of Scotland.

Ceilidh: a party with Scottish or Irish folk music and singing, traditional dancing and storytelling.

Haggis: a traditional Scottish meat dish.

Bagpipes: a musical instrument with reed pipes.

Martyr: a person who dies for their beliefs.

Shamrock: a small, three-leaved, green plant used as the national emblem of Ireland.

Your turn to speak

Discuss with your partner:

→ Have you ever stood up for someone else, or owned up to something you have done wrong?

→ Can you think of any kinds of food that are associated with other countries or traditions? For example, eating turkey at Christmas.

→ Why do you think Scottish people enjoy having their own special dances and songs?

→ Why do you think Irish people who live in other countries enjoy celebrating St Patrick's Day?

Read and understand

1. Draw a picture of the English national flag (St George's emblem of a red cross on a white background).

2. On which date is St George's Day celebrated?

3. Which flower do people wear on St George's Day?

4. What values does St George represent?

5. On which date is St David's Day celebrated?

6. What happens at an Eisteddfod?

7. What are the emblems of Wales?

8. When did St David live?

9. Draw a picture of people enjoying a ceilidh. Remember the bagpipes!

10. On which date is St Andrew's Day celebrated?

11. Who was St Andrew?

12. Describe what happens at a ceilidh.

13. On which date is St Patrick's Day celebrated?

14. Who was St Patrick? What happened to him when he was 16?

15. What is a shamrock?

16. How did St Patrick make use of the shamrock to explain ideas about Christianity? Draw a picture of a shamrock to help show what St Patrick was trying to explain.

SHARING VALUES

Sharing and commemorating special days helps us to share our beliefs and values, and make our values clear to one another.

Remembrance Day – 11 November

Remembrance Day, also known as Armistice Day, is a very special day for people throughout our country. On 11 November, many Britons wear a poppy to show that they are remembering the dead who have died for our country. Poppies were chosen because these red flowers grew up on battlefields after the First World War.

Armistice Day marks the end of the First World War in 1918, at 11am on the 11th day of the 11th month. Every year, a two-minute silence is held at 11am to remember people who have died in wars. Remembrance Sunday, which usually falls on the second Sunday in November, also gives us the chance to remember those who have died in wars, as well as the terrible loss and harm that war brings.

Harvest Festival

Harvest Festival celebrations take place towards the end of September and are celebrated in schools and churches all over Britain. They give thanks for the harvest that has been successfully grown and collected, and also celebrate all of the hard work that this has involved. Children are often encouraged to bring to school packets and tins of food that can be shared with people in the community.

Celebrating a successful harvest helps us to appreciate what we have and to remember those who are not as fortunate as we are. Harvest Festival also helps us understand that many good things need a lot of hard work and determination.

What we mean when we say...

Armistice Day: 11 November – a day to remember those who have died in wars.

Remembrance Sunday: the Sunday closest to 11 November.

Commemorating: the action of remembering and showing respect for something or someone.

Harvest Festival: a celebration of the annual harvest.

Your turn to speak

Discuss with your partner:

→ Why do you think it is important to have a special day to remember all those who have died fighting in wars?

→ What do you think you should learn from celebrating Harvest Festival?

Read and understand

1. What is the importance of the date of Armistice Day?

2. Why do people wear poppies on Remembrance Day?

3. Explain why you think it is important that we remember people who have lost their lives fighting in a war.

4. Draw a picture of your school's Harvest Festival celebrations.

5. Describe in your own words what you think people can learn by celebrating Harvest Festival.

OTHER SPECIAL DAYS AND CELEBRATIONS

Some celebrations started as a result of an event or belief, and provide very good fun for family and friends. Here are just two which you may know of:

Guy Fawkes or Bonfire Night

'Remember, remember, the fifth of November, Gunpowder, treason and plot!'

If you've ever heard this rhyme before, you will probably already know that Bonfire Night marks the discovery of a plot to blow up King James I as he opened Parliament on 5 November, 1605.

Those plotting to kill the King hid barrels of gunpowder in a cellar under the Houses of Parliament, but a secret letter warned the King and his Government about the plot. Though not the leader of the plot, Guy Fawkes was found guarding the gunpowder. After three days of torture in the Tower of London, Guy Fawkes named his fellow gang members and was then sentenced to death.

King James encouraged people to light bonfires to celebrate the failure of the plot, a tradition which survives today along with the burning of a 'Guy' on top of the fire, and big firework displays.

Chinese New Year

The date for Chinese New Year changes each year, but always falls between 21 January and 20 February.

Each new year is named after one of 12 animals in the Chinese zodiac cycle.

Many Chinese New Year celebrations take place in Britain, with special food and a lion dance.

Chinese New Year is also marked by a good deal of red lanterns, gold lettering and, of course, fireworks. Some believe that the noise of fireworks and the colour red scare away demons and evil spirits.

DO YOU REMEMBER?

Let's finish by reminding ourselves of some of the most important points we've learned:

→ Everyone is special, and everyone is important. Everybody is part of a culture and many people are part of more than one culture. Your culture is made up of everything to do with how you live.

→ Our country has been multicultural for over 2000 years. Lots of people and cultures mixing together in Britain is nothing new.

→ Everyone who has settled in the UK has brought their special cultural backgrounds.

→ Religion can be an important part of a person's cultural background. Christianity is the biggest religion in Britain.

→ Lots of people take part in Christian festivals and religions even if they are not a Christian, for example, celebrating Christmas, eating pancakes on Shrove Tuesday or giving up something for Lent.

→ Different religious festivals and traditions play a very important part in the lives of millions of people.

→ Special days celebrating the patron saints of St George, St David, St Andrew and St Patrick are also a time to celebrate the national cultures of England, Wales, Scotland and Ireland.

→ Other special days like Armistice Day (Remembrance Day) help people share important values.